The highest happiness on earth is marriage.

♥ William Lyon Phelps

The Promises of

MARRIAGE

A CELEBRATION OF THE
SPECIAL LOVE AND COMMITMENT
COUPLES SHARE

Edited by Patricia Wayant

Blue Mountain Press™
Boulder, Colorado

We wish to thank Susan Polis Schutz for permission to reprint the following poems that appear in this publication: "Love Is...," "Promises You Can Keep," "In marriage two people share...," and "I can't believe it...." Copyright © 1982, 1986, 1988, 2005 by Stephen Schutz and Susan Polis Schutz. All rights reserved.

Library of Congress Control Number: 2007908668
ISBN: 978-1-59842-314-3

Acknowledgements appear on page 92.

◪ and Blue Mountain Press are registered in U.S. Patent and Trademark Office. Certain trademarks are used under license.

Printed in China.
First Printing: 2008

✪ This book is printed on recycled paper.

This book is printed on archival quality, white felt, 110 lb. paper. This paper has been specially produced to be acid free (neutral pH) and contains no groundwood or unbleached pulp. It conforms with the requirements of the American National Standards Institute, Inc., so as to ensure that this book will last and be enjoyed by future generations.

Blue Mountain Arts, Inc.

P.O. Box 4549, Boulder, Colorado 80306

Contents

The Promises of Marriage

Marriage is...

A commitment. Its success doesn't depend on feelings, circumstances, or moods — but on two people who are loyal to each other and the vows they took on their wedding day.

Hard work. It means chores, disagreements, misunderstandings, and times when you might not like each other very much. When you work at it together, it can be the greatest blessing in the world...

Marriage is…

A relationship where two people must listen, compromise, and respect. It's an arrangement that requires a multitude of decisions to be made together. Listening, respecting, and compromising go a long way toward keeping peace and harmony.

A union in which two people learn from their mistakes, accept each other's faults, and willingly adjust behaviors that need to be changed. It's caring enough about each other to work through disappointing and hurtful times and believing in the love that brought you together in the first place.

Marriage is…

Patience and forgiveness. It's being
open and honest, thoughtful and kind.
Marriage means talking things out, making
necessary changes, and forgiving each
other. It's unconditional love at its most
understanding and vulnerable — love that
supports, comforts, and is determined to
triumph over every challenge and adversity.

Marriage is a partnership of two unique
people who bring out the very best in each
other and who know that even though they
are wonderful as individuals… they are
even better together.

♥ *Barbara Cage*

In Marriage,
Two People Can Create
an Infinite Love

When two people join together and bond their lives forever because they are certain they have something special that will make their marriage last... this is the first act of faith.

Upon this act of faith, these two people will build a life. And as long as their determination stays with them, this life will always be their hope, their dream, their truth, their being, their inspiration, and their source of strength.

Through their life together, they will hurt and laugh. Together, they will feel all of life's ups and downs. They will learn and grow through trial and error. The lessons will show them the meaning of true love and the difference between a love that lasts and one that just gives up.

These two people will face each failure together and discover the strength to go on. They will encourage each other's dreams and forgive each other's faults.

Through a labor of love, these two will become as one — fighting against the odds and ultimately creating a marriage that will grow into an infinite love.

♥ Regina Hill

We Are Not Meant to Go Through Life Alone

We need a partner in life who will
forever remain by our side —
someone to lean on at times,
remembering, as well,
that we will be leaned on, too;
someone to share our joy
and hold us in sorrow.

Understand that there will be difficult times,
and doubt may cloud your lives.
It is then that you must
trust each other the most
and believe that love will sustain you.
Do not give up easily;
fight for what is most precious —
your marriage.
Help it survive
by nurturing it every single day.

Never hesitate to say "I love you"
or be the first one to say "I'm sorry."
Give a lot,
overlook even more,
and always expect as much in return.
Never look back
or lose yourself,
but celebrate the special privilege
of being a couple.
Never lose sight
of what brought you to the altar
in the first place:
your special love for each other.
Cherish that always.

♥ *Linda Hersey*

The Magic of
Falling in Love

J can't believe it
Out of all the millions of people
in hundreds of countries
and thousands of cities
I was able to find
my true heart
my true soul
my true love

Everyone searches for love
Love unites our hearts

♥ Susan Polis Schutz

Falling in love is like being
first to discover the most beautiful
thing in the world
or to find something so lovely
that no one else had ever noticed.
It is like glimpsing the first
evening star
or the rainbow that unexpectedly
appears in the midst of a storm.

Love often starts in little ways.
It comes quietly with a smile,
a glance, or a touch,
but you know it's there
because suddenly you're not alone
and the sadness inside you is gone.
Love means finally finding a place
in this world that shelters you
and is your very own.
It's a place where you feel
you have been forever
and you live and grow and learn.

♥ *Vickie M. Worsham*

A Dream Come True

$\mathcal{J}$ used to dream
that someday I might find a lover
who would be tender, kind, and passionate,
someone whose touch
would awaken my heart
and fill me with sensations
I had only imagined
I would ever feel...
a partner who would show me
how love was meant to be.

I told myself that this was more
than I could hope for —
more than I could ever deserve.

I used to hope
that someday I might have a friend
who would know
what was deep inside my heart —
someone with whom I would be safe
to share my secrets, my dreams,
my fantasies, and my fears...
a friend whom I could always count on
to listen and to understand.

I told myself that this was
more than anyone could hope for
and much more than I
could ever be worthy of.

I never let my heart imagine
that I would find all this
    and more...
but that's what was waiting
    for me in your arms.
I found the best friend
and the best lover
that I could ever have hoped for...
    in you.

♥ *Jason Blume*

A Promise of Happiness

When I found you, I found
all the happiness that life can offer.

I found how important it is to trust
in commitment
And how wonderful it is to share
heartfelt moments with someone
so dear to you that you cannot
imagine life without them.

I found strength in companionship
And how necessary it is to be able to
lean on someone in times of need.

I found what it feels like to support
someone's hopes
And to appreciate building new
dreams together with what the
future can hold.

I found contentment in realizing that
two people can be open and honest
with each other
Without having to pretend or see
eye to eye on every subject.

I found how special it is to accept a
person for who they are
And what they can bring to your life
in expected and unexpected ways.

I found that the greatest gift anyone
can ever give to another person can
only come from the heart,
Because when I found you,
I found love.

♥ *Susan Hickman Sater*

Love Is...

Love is being happy for the other person
    when that person is happy
    being sad for the other person
    when that person is sad
    being together in good times
    and being together in bad times
Love is the source of strength

Love is being honest with yourself at all times
    being honest with the other person at all times
    telling, listening, respecting the truth
    and never pretending
Love is the source of reality

Love is an understanding so complete that
    you feel as if you are a part of the other person
    accepting that person just the way he or she is
    and not trying to change each other
    to be something else
Love is the source of unity

Love is the freedom to pursue your own desires
    while sharing your experiences with the other person
    the growth of one individual alongside of
    and together with the growth of another individual
Love is the source of success

Love is the excitement of planning things together
    the excitement of doing things together
Love is the source of the future

Love is the fury of the storm
    the calm in the rainbow
Love is the source of passion

Love is giving and taking in a daily situation
    being patient with each other's needs and desires
Love is the source of sharing

Love is knowing that the other person
    will always be with you regardless of what happens
    missing the other person when he or she is away
    but remaining near in heart at all times
Love is the source of security

Love is the source of life

♥ Susan Polis Schutz

From This Day Forward

From this day forward,
you shall not walk alone.
My heart will be your shelter,
and my arms will be your home.

♥ *Author Unknown*

Remember that the first step
        begins any journey…
    setting the course,
        mapping out your future,
choosing the direction you will follow
    as husband and wife.
Remember that each road,
        no matter how straight it seems,
    has bumps and detours.
No matter how perfect your plans are laid,
        the course can change
    when you least expect it.
But whatever bump or hill or detour
        you experience on your journey,
    it will only enhance the trip.
Do not be stopped by a change in plans.
Remember that a delay can offer
        a chance to explore territory
    you might not otherwise have seen.
The best part of the trip is the journey,
    not the destination.
You have the keys to each other's heart in hand.
Your road to happiness
        and a successful life together begins
    with the first step on the day you wed.
May every road you follow
    lead you to another memory.

♥ *Linda Robertson*

To My Bride

I want to walk life's path with you by my side. I want us to be together, because I love you and because being with you seems more meant to be than anything that's ever happened to me.

I want to go places with you. I want us to set off to see what's at the end of every rainbow. But we don't have to go adventuring miles and miles away. There's a lot to see right here, close to home. Close to you. I want us to discover that the single best place in the world is wherever we are… when we're together.

I want us to have a deeper and sweeter understanding than we've ever known before. I want us to talk things over, whether they're little or large, and say all the things that we want to share. I want us to have a direct connection, heart-to-heart, and to have the open, easy, caring kind of communication that keeps people so close and makes them so happy inside. And…

I want to love you for the rest of my life.

♥ *M. Best*

To My Groom

$\mathcal{I}$ want to love you soul to soul in the deepest, most unspoken places forever.

I want to love you bigger than borders… higher than mountains… and longer than the lonely hours.

I want to fly with you over the back-alley gravel trails of the world, spinning our golden thread through big city rush-hour tangles and rain-rutted country downtown corners.

I want to watch the day awaken from the stronghold of your embrace and fall asleep to the lullaby of gentle in-and-out breathings that rise and fall on the tide of your chest.

I want to know you by heart: looks, gestures, thoughts; all the stories that sewn together make up the fabric of your spirit; all the loves and hates that spark your soul.

I want to love you heart to heart… forever.

♥ Shawnacy Perez

A Marriage Blessing

because everyone knows exactly what's good for another
because very few see
because a man and a woman may just possibly look at each
       other
because in the insanity of human relationships there still
       may come a time we say: yes, yes
because a man or a woman can do anything he or she
       pleases
because you can reach any point in your life saying: now, i
       want this
because eventually it occurs we want each other, we want
       to know each other, even stupidly, even uglily
because there is at best a simple need in two people to try
       and reach some simple ground
because that simple ground is not so simple
because we are human beings gathered together whether
       we like it or not
because we are human beings reaching out to touch
because sometimes we grow

       we ask a blessing on this marriage
       we ask that some simplicity be allowed
       we ask their happiness
       we ask that this couple be known for what it is,
          and that the light shine upon it
       we ask a blessing for their marriage

♥ Joel Oppenheimer

The Art of Marriage

Happiness in marriage is not something that just happens. A good marriage must be created. In the art of marriage the *little things* are the *big things*...

It is never being too old to hold hands.

It is remembering to say, "I love you," at least once each day.

It is never going to sleep angry.

It is at no time taking the other for granted; the courtship shouldn't end with the honeymoon, it should continue through all the years.

It is having a mutual sense of values and common objectives; it is standing together facing the world.

It is forming a circle of love that gathers in the whole family.

It is doing things for each other, not in the attitude of duty or sacrifice, but in the spirit of joy.

It is speaking words of appreciation and demonstrating gratitude in thoughtful ways.

It is not expecting the husband to wear a halo or the wife to have the wings of an angel. It is not looking for perfection in each other. It is cultivating flexibility, patience, understanding and a sense of humor.

It is having the capacity to forgive and forget.

It is giving each other an atmosphere in which each can grow.

It is finding room for the things of the spirit. It is a common search for the good and the beautiful.

It is not only marrying the right partner, it is *being* the right partner.

♥ *Wilferd A. Peterson*

When Two
Become One

 $\mathcal{W}$ hat greater thing is there for two human souls than to feel that they are joined for life — to strengthen each other in all labor, to rest on each other in all sorrow, to minister to each other in all pain, to be one with each other in silent, unspeakable memories.

♥ *George Eliot*

ı carry your heart with me(i carry it in
my heart)i am never without it(anywhere
i go you go,my dear;and whatever is done
by only me is your doing,my darling)

　　　　　　　　　　　　　i fear
no fate(for you are my fate,my sweet)i want
no world(for beautiful you are my world,my true)
and it's you are whatever a moon has always meant
and whatever a sun will always sing is you

here is the deepest secret nobody knows
(here is the root of the root and the bud of the bud
and the sky of the sky of a tree called life;which grows
higher than soul can hope or mind can hide)
and this is the wonder that's keeping the stars apart

i carry your heart(i carry it in my heart)

♥ E. E. Cummings

True Love Is "We" Instead of "Me"

True love is being the best of friends — being able to say and share anything while still being sensitive to the other's feelings.

True love is built upon complete trust — complete by knowing that you can never be deceitful or misleading, because to do so would forever cloud the relationship with doubt.

True love is knowing that you'd rather be with this other person more than anyone else, and you feel a sense of emptiness when the two of you are apart.

It's when you always think of the future in terms of "we" instead of "me."

True love is treasuring the touch of the other person while feeling a sense of contentment and completeness as you emotionally and physically embrace.

It is wanting to make the other person happy and fulfilled in every possible way while doing everything you can to prevent their distress.

True love is a commitment to working out the differences that will always come about when two people become one.

It is knowing that life will bring pain and sorrow, but together, you will support each other and overcome even the most difficult times.

True love is showing and saying "I love you" even when you both know — through a simple smile — that doing so isn't necessary.

True love is complete within itself, and it lasts into eternity.

♥ *Jim Tweedie*

Soul Mates

Somewhere there waiteth in this world of ours
For one lone soul another lonely soul,
Each chasing each through all the weary hours
And meeting strangely at one sudden goal;
Then blend they like green leaves with autumn flowers
Into one beautiful and perfect whole;
And life's long night is ended, and the way
Lies open, onward to eternal day.

♥ *Sir Edwin Arnold*

A soulmate is someone who has locks that fit our keys, and keys to fit our locks. When we feel safe enough to open the locks, our truest selves step out and we can be completely and honestly who we are; we can be loved for who we are and not for who we're pretending to be. Each unveils the best part of the other. No matter what else goes wrong around us, with that one person we're safe in our own paradise. Our soulmate is someone who shares our deepest longing, our sense of direction. When we're two balloons, and together our direction is up, chances are we've found the right person. Our soulmate is the one who makes life come to life.

♥ *Richard Bach*

From every human being there rises a light that reaches straight to heaven. And when two souls that are destined to be together find each other, their streams of light flow together, and a single brighter light goes forth from their united being.

♥ *Baal Shem Tov*

You and I

You and I
Have so much love,
That it
Burns like a fire,
In which we bake a lump of clay
Molded into a figure of you
And a figure of me.
Then we take both of them,
And break them into pieces,
And mix the pieces with water,
And mold again a figure of you,
And a figure of me.
I am in your clay.
You are in my clay.
In life we share a single quilt.
In death we will share one coffin.

♥ Kuan Tao-shêng

$\mathcal{J}$ do not love you as if you were salt-rose,
   or topaz,
or the arrow of carnations the fire shoots off.
I love you as certain dark things are to be loved,
in secret, between the shadow and the soul.

I love you as the plant that never blooms
but carries in itself the light of hidden flowers;
thanks to your love a certain solid fragrance,
risen from the earth, lives darkly in my body.

I love you without knowing how, or when,
   or from where.
I love you straightforwardly, without complexities
   or pride;
so I love you because I know no other way

than this: where *I* does not exist, nor *you*,
so close that your hand on my chest is my hand,
so close that your eyes close as I fall asleep.

♥ *Pablo Neruda*

Marriage Is a
Beautiful Union of
Friendship and Love

Marriage in the best times is a complete synchronicity, full of joy and significance. At its worst, it is a test of character, selflessness, and maturity. It is the assurance of keeping promises. It is embarking on a lifetime journey as partners, lovers, and allies. It is a union based on the belief that marriage, unlike so many things today, is not returnable or exchangeable.

Marriage understands that romance is fleeting and commitment is binding. It is a love that embraces flaws and forgives; it knows that differences are healthy guideposts for respect, encouragement, and friendship.

A marriage that lasts isn't a matter of luck or whether your love is deep enough. Rather, it is a matter of carefully preserving each other's individual dreams and desires without losing them to the shadow of fear, jealousy, and prejudice.

Marriage is a partnership — woven together by the strands of love and secured by the clasp of friendship.

♥ *Lisa Crofton*

A Promise to Be Together Always

We belong together
because whenever you smile,
something deep inside me
urges me to smile back;
whenever I'm down
and I hear your laughter,
I come alive again.

Whenever I get too excited or agitated,
you know how to calm me down.
I often catch myself
watching your face as you talk
or when you listen to others,
and just seeing your reactions
makes me happy.

Whenever we talk you'll say something
that has been asleep in me for a while —
or even something I never knew was there.
You're the first person
I want to see in the morning
and the last one I want to touch
before I go to sleep.

You're the one I want to turn to
when things get rough;
the one I want to share
my happiness with
when things are going great;
the one to whom I want to entrust
my dreams and my heart.

I know we belong together because
I have a faith in you
unlike the faith I have in anyone else;
because you bring out the best in me,
just as I bring it out in you.

I know we belong together because
I want to love you
and do for you all that love entails.
I want your happiness as much as
I want my own, if not more,
and this desire will never go away.

♥ Christine Nemec

Promises You Can Keep

I cannot promise you that
I will not change
I cannot promise you that
I will not have many different moods
I cannot promise you that
I will not hurt your feelings sometimes
I cannot promise you that
I will not be erratic
I cannot promise you that
I will always be strong
I cannot promise you that
my faults will not show

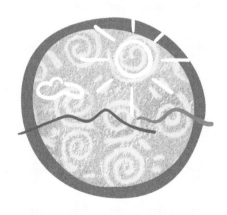

But —

I do promise you that

I will always be supportive of you

I do promise you that

I will share all my thoughts

  and feelings with you

I do promise you that

I will give you freedom to be yourself

I do promise you that

I will understand everything that you do

I do promise you that

I will be completely honest with you

I do promise you that

I will laugh and cry with you

I do promise you that

I will help you achieve all your goals

But —

most of all

I do promise you that

I will love you

♥ *Susan Polis Schutz*

Why Marriage?

A marriage is risky business these days
Says some old and prudent voice inside.
We don't need twenty children anymore
To keep the family line alive,
Or gather up the hay before the rain.
No law demands respectability.
Love can arrive without certificate or cash.
History and experience both make clear
That men and women do not hear
The music of the world in the same key,
Rather rolling dissonances doomed to clash.

So what is left to justify a marriage?
Maybe only the hunch that half the world
Will ever be present in any room
With just a single pair of eyes to see it.
Whatever is invisible to one
Is to the other an enormous golden lion
Calm and sleeping in the easy chair.
After many years, if things go right
Both lion and emptiness are always there;
The one never true without the other.

But the dark secret of the ones long married,
A pleasure never mentioned to the young,
Is the sweet heat made from two bodies in a bed
Curled together on a winter night,
The smell of the other always in the quilt,
The hand set quietly on the other's flank
That carries news from another world
Light-years away from the one inside
That you always thought you inhabited alone.
The heat in that hand could melt a stone.

 Bill Holm

The Best Things About Marriage

*Y*ou go home. You find little things to cherish. You have a favorite chair. You develop a coffee ritual, a storybook ritual, some running jokes. From little things emerges something big, and you realize that being married with kids is the essential condition of your life, an immutable fact, something you don't ever want to change.

Just like true love.

♥ *Joel Achenbach*

$\mathcal{I}$n marriage
two people share
all their dreams and goals
their weaknesses and strengths
In marriage
two people share
all the joys and sadnesses of life
and all the supreme pleasures
In marriage
two people share
all of their emotions and feelings
all of their tears and laughter

Marriage is the most
fulfilling relationship
one can have
and the love that you share
as husband and wife
is beautifully forever

♥ *Susan Polis Schutz*

"The Marriage Poem"

Being married is the most wonderful thing that can happen to two people in love ♥ A marriage is a caring commitment to making a miracle last forever ♥ It truthfully whispers the words "I don't know what I'd ever do without you" ♥ It joyfully says "I want you to be there in all my tomorrows" ♥ And it sings the praises of sharing life, as husband and wife, sweetly and completely together ♥ A marriage is opening the door to all the good things and best wishes around you ♥ A marriage is opening your hearts to the wonders within you ♥ A marriage is a promise to stay together, to dream together, to work on whatever needs attention, to keep love fresh and alive, and to continue to bless the beauty of your lives ♥ A marriage is reaching for the wishes you both want to come true and remembering the priceless smiles that come from hearing "I love you" ♥

A marriage is one of life's most wondrous blessings ♥ It involves taking the words of two life stories and weaving them together on the same pages ♥ Every year, in a thousand special ways, the words that will be written in this remarkable story will reflect the strength and the joy and the love that rises above any trials and sorrows ♥ A marriage is the precious, reassuring comfort of having a kindred soul care about your day, every day and each tomorrow, your whole life long ♥

A marriage is the making of a home that seems so meant to be… between a special woman and a special man ♥ A marriage is a beautiful journey along life's road with two people smiling as they go, lovingly… hand in hand ♥

♥ *Douglas Pagels*

What Is a Husband?

He's more myself than I am. Whatever our souls are made of, his and mine are the same... If all else perished and *he* remained, I should still continue to be, and if all else remained, and he were annihilated, the universe would turn to a might stranger... He's always, always in my mind; not as a pleasure to myself, but as my own being.

♥ *Emily Brontë*

$\mathcal{A}$ husband is a man
who overlooks your bad points,
but doesn't overlook you.
He's someone who can
make you feel beautiful
by a look in his eyes.
He knows when to wrap his arms around you
to shield you from the world
and when to leave you alone
if you need some space.
He gives you the freedom
to be your own person,
but is always available
so that you're never alone.
He shares what goes on in his life
and cares about what goes on in yours.
He's a part of you;
he's always on your mind
and in your heart.
A husband is an irreplaceable
person in your life —
he's a lover, a protector,
a companion, and a friend.

♥ Barbara Cage

To My Kind
and Gentle Husband

 When I look in your eyes... I see all the things that you are — kindness, gentleness, compassion, and love. There's a twinkle that sometimes appears when you are talking about the beautiful things in this world that are so important to you.

When I hear your voice... I hear the sweetest sound I have ever heard. When you say, "I love you," it touches me in a way no other words ever have or ever will touch me again.

When I see your face... I see a man who has so much depth. Your face reflects a bittersweet past and holds so much hope for the future. It's an honest and trusting face, with a boyish quality that is so rare in a world that makes us grow old before our time.

When you hold me… you have a way like magic of making me feel so peaceful, secure, and content with my world and everything that is around me. Life is a wonderland in your arms — a place I thought I would never find.

When you love me… that is the greatest gift of all. You give me an unselfish, undemanding, uninhibited kind of love that I thought only existed in my dreams. You have filled an empty space inside me, and now I feel that I am complete.

Your love has given me life, and now, with you, my life is full of love.

♥ *Marianne Freeman*

What Is a Wife?

A wife cares for your soul, nurtures your heart, and teaches you the purity and strength of an unconditional love.

♥ *Tim M. Krzys*

A wife is someone more special than words. She's love mixed with friendship and marriage bonded with hope, thanks, and joy. A wife is beauty and lasting togetherness, and there is no one more precious in the world.

A wife is one who inspires some of the most special moments two people have ever shared. A wife is a treasured perspective on the past, a reassuring part of the present, and a million wishes for all the days that lie ahead.

A wife is a reminder of the blessings that come from closeness. Sharing everything. Disclosing dreams. Learning about life together. She's a hand within your hand and often the only one who understands. A wife is understanding and trust enfolded with love. She is a helper and a guide, and she is a feeling deep inside that makes you realize, each and every day of your life, that there is no one who could ever be loved in the way a husband... loves his wife.

♥ *C. Martin*

To My Beautiful and Loving Wife

Our wedding vows are engraved on my heart. They are more than spoken words that echo in our past. These words are the foundation of who I am and what our love means to me. They are an expression of my love and my commitment to you and us.

Marriage brings deep joy and the seeds of everlasting happiness. It is the result of two souls intermingling that grow together with the passage of time. It creates a bedrock foundation of strength and a shield against the challenges inherent in life as we compromise, understand, and forgive. It allows us to make mistakes, to fail and falter, to be hurt and yet grow and thrive in the warming light of forgiveness.

Our wedding vows illustrate my position in life beside you — neither a follower nor a leader, but an equal with my hand in yours. We are partners in all we do; we have more strength together than we do as individuals. I trust in the strength and commitment of our marriage; I have faith and ask for nothing else.

I'm here forever as your husband, best friend and supporter, love and life partner. The vows we exchanged are not merely words; they are me and everything I hope to be. They are a part of my love, a part of my soul, and forever a part of my heart.

♥ *Tim M. Krzys*

The Bonds of Marriage

arriage is the joining of two people
who share the promise that only marriage
can make — to share the sunshine and the
shadows and to experience a richer, more
fulfilling life because of it.

♥ *Bettie Meeks*

Marriage, which is always spoken of as a bond, becomes actually many bonds, many strands, of different texture and strength, making up a web that is taut and firm. The web is fashioned of love. Yes, but many kinds of love: romantic love first, then a slow-growing devotion and, playing through these, a constantly rippling companionship. It is made of loyalties, and interdependencies, and shared experiences. It is woven of memories of meetings and conflicts; of triumphs and disappointments. It is a web of communication, a common language, and the acceptance of lack of language, too; a knowledge of likes and dislikes, of habits and reactions, both physical and mental. It is a web of instincts and intuitions, and known and unknown exchanges. The web of marriage is made by propinquity, in the day to day living side by side, looking outward and working outward in the same direction. It is woven in space and in time of the substance of life itself.

♥ *Anne Morrow Lindberg*

Marriage Is like the Planting of Two Trees...

*L*et them take root in soil made fertile with love, understanding, and respect.

Let them grow tall to give each other shade from the sun. Let neither seek to overshadow the other, but let them grow strong together as equals.

Let their branches intertwine to give each other support and provide shelter for those who come beneath their shade.

If storm winds break their branches, let them have the inner vitality of love and faith to grow new branches and be even stronger than before.

And let them stand like oaks for many years together and pass on their strength and beauty for generations to come.

♥ *Moira Allen*

Tree Marriage

In Chota Nagpur and Bengal
the betrothed are tied with threads to
mango trees, they marry the trees
as well as one another, and
the two trees marry each other.
Could we do that some time with oaks
or beeches? This gossamer we
hold each other with, this web
of love and habit is not enough.
In mistrust of heavier ties,
I would like tree-siblings for us,
standing together somewhere, two
trees married with us, lightly, their
fingers barely touching in sleep,
our threads invisible but holding.

♥ *William Meredith*

In Marriage,
Cherish Each Other
in Big Ways and in
Small Ways

Remember that it is the little things
that make the difference...
Don't forget the birthdays
and the anniversaries.
An occasional note means a lot.
Share each other's life —
even the small details —
far too often we forget
that day-after-day becomes year-after-year,
and then it's gone.
Give each other room to grow...
We all need our time alone.
Keep strong your faith in each other;
time has a funny way of testing us,
and it's faith that gets us through.
Respect each other...
This world could always use more of that.
Speak your mind honestly, openly,
but with kindness,
for angry words are scars
that may never heal.
Trust each other;
let your trust be your rock.
Most of all, each day...
be sure to hold each other
and fall in love all over again.

♥ Julia Escobar

The ABC's of a Good Relationship

Always listen with your heart. Hear more than just what is being said.

Believe in yourself. Be understanding and accepting. No two people are alike; see each other's point of view.

Communicate. As much as we'd like them to be, our partners aren't mind readers. Open up and don't be afraid to show your true feelings. Create an atmosphere where feelings are accepted and talked about.

Don't judge. Accept the other for who they are — the unique individual you fell in love with.

Expect happiness. Have fun. Allow humor to get you through some of life's stresses.

Fear nothing. Trust in each other and
the love you share. Together you can
do anything.

Give of yourself: your time, your energy,
your affection.

Help whenever you can by listening, caring,
and doing.

Initiate affection, laughter, fun, and play.

Just be yourself. Don't ever pretend to be
what you aren't.

Kiss and make up. Don't hold a grudge.
Forgive and forget.

Love unconditionally, patiently, passionately,
hopefully, and enduringly.

(If you can do all of these, you don't need
the rest of the alphabet!)

♥ *Barbara Cage*

No One Ever Said Marriage Is Easy

We've sure found that out.
But we've also learned
that getting past
the hard times
has made us stronger,
and it has made us
love each other more
than we ever thought possible.

♥ *Marijoe Young*

$\mathcal{M}$arriage is serious business and hard work. It's not just becoming roommates, it's becoming soul mates; it's not just signing a license, it's sharing a life.... The words in the marriage ceremony "from this day forward" *are* scary. At the moment a couple exchanges those vows, they can never know what they really mean, what hills and valleys stretch out in front of them in the years ahead. But if you take the words seriously, there's no going back. There's only the future, unlimited and unknowable, and the promise to make the journey together.

♥ *Cokie and Steve Roberts*

$\mathcal{B}$etween a man and his wife nothing ought rule but love. As love ought to bring them together, so it is the best way to keep them well together.

♥ *William Penn*

Marriage Advice

*L*et your love be stronger than your hate and anger.
Learn the wisdom of compromise,
for it is better to bend a little than to break.
Believe the best rather than the worst.
People have a way of living up or down
to your opinion of them.
Remember that true friendship is the basis
for any lasting relationship.
The person you choose to marry
is deserving of the courtesies and kindnesses
you bestow on your friends.

 *Jane Wells*

$\mathcal{W}$ork slowly with each other and build a relationship that you both can enjoy being a part of.

Share love and understand that neither of you is perfect; you are both subject to human frailties.

Encourage each other to pursue your dreams, even when you're weary from trying.

Expect the best that you both have to give, and still love when you fall short of your expectations.

Be friends; respect each other's individual personality, and give each other room to grow.

Be candid with each other, and point out strengths and weaknesses.

Understand each other's personal philosophy, even if you don't agree.

Be friends as well as lovers.

♥ *Denise Braxton-Brown*

"Let There Be Spaces in Your Togetherness"

*Y*ou were born together, and together
you shall be forevermore.

You shall be together when the white wings
of death scatter your days.

Ay, you shall be together even in the silent
memory of God.

But let there be spaces in your togetherness,

And let the winds of the heavens dance
between you.

Love one another, but make not a bond of love:

Let it rather be a moving sea between the shores of your souls.

Fill each other's cup but drink not from one cup.

Give one another of your bread but eat not from the same loaf.

Sing and dance together and be joyous, but let each one of you be alone,

Even as the strings of a lute are alone though they quiver with the same music.

Give your hearts, but not into each other's keeping.

For only the hand of Life can contain your hearts.

And stand together yet not too near together:

For the pillars of the temple stand apart,

And the oak tree and the cypress grow not in each other's shadow.

♥ *Kahlil Gibran*

Marriage Is a Journey You Take Together

*A*s you travel down the road of life,
May you always walk hand in hand.
There will be many lessons ahead of you —
Some happy, some difficult —
But may you always turn to
     each other for support.
May there be lots of happiness
     and laughter to celebrate together.
May you support and respect
     each other's dreams
And then stand back and watch them
     come true.
During the difficult times,
Hold each other a little tighter,
Love a little more,
And know that you don't have to
     go through anything alone —
For you have each other,
Now and for always.

If you ever find that you are no longer
    walking side by side,
Don't walk away.
Stop and reach back to let the other
Know you are there
And always will be.
Wake up each morning and be
    thankful for each other,
For love is a gift;
It is the only thing that is real,
The only thing we keep and take with us.
Hold each other tightly
And never let go,
For this is a journey to be taken together.

♥ *Erin McGraw*

A Promise to Love
Each Other
No Matter What

Despite any obstacles
that come our way
and all the many differences we will share,
I will always love you...

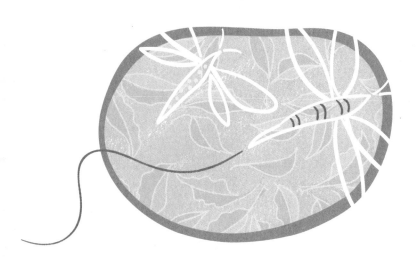

I will love you when our moods vary
and when our opinions go
    in opposite directions.
I will love you when your ideas
    aren't quite the same as mine
        and our beliefs clash.
I will love you when you take a stand
    on what you feel is absolutely right,
even if I don't feel the same.
I will even love you when you're tired
    and grumpy
and don't want much to do with me
    at that moment.
I will love you no matter what,
even as we struggle to be
    our own individuals.
It doesn't matter how different we may be.
I will love you most of all because
you are different from me
    and can express it.

I love you for what you believe,
    for the emotions you feel,
and for the ideas that help me
    open my own mind
to possibilities I haven't yet explored.

♥ *Beverly K. Metott*

10 Golden Rules for Staying Happily Married

1. First and foremost, love each other. Say "I love you" often and in different ways. Do things to keep your love and romance new and alive. Don't take love for granted, ever.

2. Listen objectively to each other, and accept each other completely. Give each other the right to disagree and to have different opinions.

3. Never stop treating each other like sweethearts. Talk to each other as sweethearts, and do things that sweethearts do. Don't let external values have more importance than the internal feelings of your heart.

4. Take care of each other. Put the other one first, but don't neglect your own needs either. Do the things that show that you're interested in your partner's needs, desires, and problems.

5. Be joyful that you've each made a commitment to the other… through sickness and health and everything else. Be thankful you're in this life together.

6. Talk about things together. Refuse to say anything negative about your partner. Never betray each other's secrets. Keep your own identity, but walk together as one.

7. Settle the fact that you've made your choice and you're no longer looking for anyone else. Don't flirt. Think of the consequences. Don't consider it.

8. Be in agreement about how your money is spent. Big items should have the approval of both. Talk about how to manage your finances.

9. Treat each other as you would want to be treated. If you've argued, never go to sleep without asking the other's forgiveness. Be faithful about this. Do what will make you both the happiest and be the best for your marriage.

10. Have fun!

♥ *Donna Fargo*

A Promise to Comfort
and Support

We seek the comfort of another. Someone to share and share the life we choose. Someone to help us through the never ending attempt to understand ourselves. And in the end, someone to comfort us along the way.

♥ *Marlin Finch Lupus*

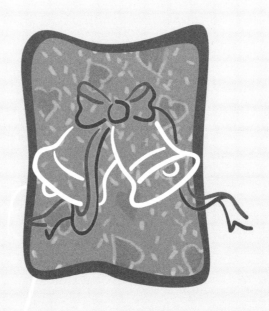

A Marriage

You are holding up a ceiling
with both arms. It is very heavy,
but you must hold it up, or else
it will fall down on you. Your arms
are tired, terribly tired,
and, as the day goes on, it feels
as if either your arms or the ceiling
will soon collapse.

But then,
unexpectedly,
something wonderful happens:
Someone,
a man or a woman,
walks into the room
and holds their arms up
to the ceiling beside you.

So you finally get
to take down your arms.
You feel the relief of respite,
the blood flowing back
to your fingers and arms.
And when your partner's arms tire,
you hold up your own
to relieve him again.

And it can go on like this
for many years
without the house falling.

♥ *Michael Blumenthal*

It's What You Give to Each Other Every Day

You can give without loving, but you can never love without giving. The great acts of love are done by those who are habitually performing small acts of kindness. We pardon to the extent that we love. Love is knowing that even when you are alone, you will never be lonely again. The greatest happiness of life is the conviction that we are loved — loved for ourselves, or rather, loved in spite of ourselves.

♥ *Victor Hugo*

For true love is inexhaustible; the more you give, the more you have. And if you go to draw at the true fountainhead, the more water you draw, the more abundant is its flow.

♥ *Antoine de Saint-Exupéry*

The meaning of marriage begins in the giving of words. We cannot join ourselves to one another without giving our word. And this must be an unconditional giving, for in joining ourselves to one another we join ourselves to the unknown. We can join one another *only* by joining the unknown. We must not be misled by the procedures of experimental thought: in life, in the world, we are never given two known results to choose between, but only *one* result that we choose without knowing what it is....

Because the condition of marriage is worldly and its meaning communal, no one party to it can be solely in charge. What you alone think it ought to be, it is not going to be. Where you alone think you want it to go, it is not going to go. It is going where the two of you — and marriage, time, life, history, and the world — will take it. You do not know the road; you have committed your life to a way.

♥ *Wendell Berry*

Remember the Promise of Your Wedding Vows

True love is never perfect.
You will argue, fight, complain,
   and blame.
But the promise of
your wedding vows —
to love, honor, and cherish
   each other —
overcomes all your conflicts
and reminds you to stop
   and count your blessings.

Your love is as strong
as the promise you made
to each other
the day you were married.
And in the turbulence
of the worst storms,
your true love
will always stand tall.

You will keep on surviving
and thriving
in your garden of real-life
    togetherness.
And the beautiful thing
is that you will not only survive,
but bloom magnificently —
because you are
always in love with each other.

♥ Jacqueline Schiff

Cherish Your Time Together

*W*hether you are spending time at home, vacationing, or doing simple, everyday things, love your times together. You are blessed to be married to your best friend... the one you turn to when things in your life are going wrong and you need an understanding heart... the one who always stands beside you — never questioning whether or not you will be there. This person is the most faithful, loyal friend you will ever know. Tell this person how much you love being married to him or her.

♥ *Cheryl E. Smith*

$\mathcal{E}$njoy the good times...
but be there for each other
   at all times.
Make yourself, as well as your partner,
   happy,
and let them find their own
   happiness, too.
Share all things; learn new things.
Always remember the times when you
   first fell in love
and all the special moments.
Keep making every year special,
and always love each other.

   ♥ *Carol Krawchuk-Howard*

Forever and Ever...

Grow old with me!
The best is yet to be.

♥ *Robert Browning*

The question is asked: "Is there anything more beautiful in life than a young couple clasping clean hands and pure hearts in the path of marriage? Can there be anything more beautiful than young love?"

And the answer is given: "Yes, there is a more beautiful thing. It is the spectacle of an old man and an old woman finishing their journey together on that path. Their hands are gnarled but still clasped; their faces are seamed but still radiant; their hearts are physically bowed and tired but still strong with love and devotion. Yes, there is a more beautiful thing than young love. Old love.

♥ *Author Unknown*

The most wonderful of all things in life is the discovery of another human being with whom one's relationship has a glowing depth, beauty, and joy as the years increase.

♥ *Sir Hugh Walpole*

A Promise to Be Together Always

I want to grow old with you,
lose count of the sunsets we share,
stroll along a moonlit beach —
always holding hands
and looking into each other's eyes
with deep longing —
no matter our age.

I want memories of sitting by a campfire,
warm conversation filling the
crisp forest air between us,
and evening whispers among the trees
filling my soul with love for you.
I want to wake beside you each morning
and feel the brightness and warmth
of your sunshine on my face.
I want to travel the world
with you beside me,
explore the space between our souls,
and feel the ever-growing love
that feeds our spirits.

I want to feel the universe between us,
sit beneath the clear evening sky,
imagine heaven, and thank God for
the gift of you.
I want to play in the snow,
make angels, and write messages of love
with my gloved hand.

I want to face the challenge of conveying
to you this deepening love I have.
Trying to tell you how much
I love you is like translating
beautiful music into something
that is still and silent —
yet I shall always make the effort,
though it seems as impossible as
describing heaven.

I want you beside me
as my best friend and lover.
Always.
I want you forever with me,
forever soul mates,
today and always…
beyond tomorrow.

♥ *Tim M. Krzys*

Marriage
Is a Promise
of Love

Marriage is a commitment to life — to the best that two people can find and bring out in each other. It offers opportunities for sharing and growth no other human relationship can equal, a physical and emotional joining that is promised for a lifetime.

Within the circle of its love, marriage encompasses all of life's most important relationships. A wife and husband are each other's best friend, confidant, lover, teacher, listener, and critic. There may come times when one partner is heartbroken or ailing, and the love of the other may resemble the tender caring of a parent for a child.

Marriage deepens and enriches every facet of life. Happiness is fuller; memories are fresher; commitment is stronger; even anger is felt more strongly and passes away more quickly.

Marriage understands and forgives the mistakes life is unable to avoid. It encourages and nurtures new life, new experiences, and new ways of expressing love through the seasons of life.

When two people pledge to love and care for each other in marriage, they create a spirit unique to themselves, which binds them closer than any spoken or written words. Marriage is a promise, a potential, made in the hearts of two people who love, which takes a lifetime to fulfill.

♥ *Edmund O'Neill*

ACKNOWLEDGMENTS

We gratefully acknowledge the permission granted by the following authors, publishers, and authors' representatives to reprint poems or excerpts from their publications.

Jason Blume for "A Dream Come True." Copyright © 2002 by Jason Blume. All rights reserved.

Shawnacy Perez for "To My Bridegroom." Copyright © 2008 by Shawnacy Perez. All rights reserved.

Theresa Maier for "because everyone knows exactly..." from "A Prayer" from ON OCCASION: SOME BIRTHS, DEATHS, WEDDINGS, BIRTHDAYS, HOLIDAYS, AND OTHER EVENTS by Joel Oppenheimer. Copyright © 1973 by Joel Oppenheimer. All rights reserved.

Heacock Literary Agency, Inc., for "The Art of Marriage" from THE ART OF LIVING by Wilferd A. Peterson. Copyright © 1960, 1961 by Wilferd A. Peterson. All rights reserved.

Liveright Publishing Corporation for "i carry your heart with me..." from COMPLETE POEMS: 1904-1962 by E. E. Cummings, edited by George J. Firmage. Copyright 1952, © 1980, 1991 by the Trustees for the E. E. Cummings Trust. Used by permissions. All rights reserved.

HarperCollins Publishers for "A soulmate is someone who has..." from THE BRIDGE ACROSS FOREVER: A LOVESTORY by Richard Bach. Copyright © 1984, 2006 by Alternate Futures Incorporated. All rights reserved.

New Directions Publishing Corp. for "You and I" by Kuan Tao-shêng from WOMEN POETS OF CHINA, translated by Kenneth Rexroth and Ling Chung. Copyright © 1973 by Kenneth Rexroth and Ling Chung. All rights reserved.

University of Texas Press for "I do not love you as if you were..." from 100 LOVE SONNETS by Pablo Neruda, translated by Stephen Tapscott. Copyright © 1959 by Pablo Neruda and Heirs of Pablo Neruda. Translation copyright © 1986 by the University of Texas Press. All rights reserved.

Lisa Crofton for "Marriage Is a Beautiful Union of Friendship and Love." Copyright © 2008 by Lisa Crofton. All rights reserved.

Milkweed Editions for "A marriage is risky business..." from "Wedding Poem" from PLAYING THE BLACK PIANO by Bill Holm. Copyright © 2004 by Bill Holm. All rights reserved.

Joel Achenbach for "You go home...." Copyright © 1999 by Joel Achenbach. All rights reserved.

Pantheon Books, a division of Random House, Inc., for "Marriage, which is always spoken of..." from GIFT FROM THE SEA by Anne Morrow Lindbergh. Copyright © 1955, 1975 by Anne Morrow Lindbergh. Copyright renewed 1983 by Anne Morrow Lindbergh. All rights reserved.

Moira Allen for "Marriage Is like the Planting of Two Trees." Copyright © 2008 by Moira Allen. All rights reserved.

Northwestern University Press for "Tree Marriage" from EFFORT AT SPEECH by William Meredith. Copyright © 1997 by William Meredith. All rights reserved.

William Morrow and Company, a division of HarperCollins Publishers, for "Marriage is serious business..." from FROM THIS DAY FORWARD by Cokie and Steve Roberts. Copyright © 2000 by Cokie and Steven V. Roberts. All rights reserved.

Alfred A. Knopf, a division of Random House, Inc., for "You were born together..." from THE PROPHET by Kahlil Gibran. Copyright 1923 by Kahlil Gibran. Renewal copyright 1951 by Administrators C.T.A. of Kahlil Gibran Estate, and Mary G. Gibran. All rights reserved.

Erin McGraw for "Marriage Is a Journey You Take Together." Copyright © 2008 by Erin McGraw. All rights reserved.

PrimaDonna Entertainment Corp. for "10 Golden Rules for Staying Happily Married" by Donna Fargo. Copyright © 2000 by PrimaDonna Entertainment Corp. All rights reserved.

Viking, a division of Penguin Group (USA), Inc., for "A Marriage" from AGAINST ROMANCE by Michael Blumenthal. Copyright © 1987 by Michael Blumenthal. All rights reserved.

Harcourt, Inc., for "For true love is..." from THE WISDOM OF THE SANDS by Antoine de Saint-Exupéry. Copyright © 1950 by Harcourt, Brace and Company, Inc. All rights reserved.

Wendell Berry for "The meaning of marriage begins in..." from STANDING BY WORDS, published by North Point Press. Copyright © 1983 by Wendell Berry. Reprinted by permission. All rights reserved.

A careful effort has been made to trace the ownership of selections used in this anthology in order to obtain permission to reprint copyrighted material and give proper credit to the copyright owners. If any error or omission has occurred, it is completely inadvertent, and we would like to make corrections in future editions provided that written notification is made to the publisher:

BLUE MOUNTAIN ARTS, INC., P.O. Box 4549, Boulder, Colorado 80306.